# SWATCHES

## Poems
## by
## Erik La Prade

POETS WEAR PRADA • Hoboken, New Jersey

# SWATCHES

First North American Publication 2008.

Copyright © 2008 Erik La Prade

http://pwpbooks.blogspot.com/

Grateful acknowledgment is made to the following publications where some of these poems have previously appeared:

| | |
|---|---|
| *Artist and Influence* | "A Bad Record" |
| *The Reading Room* | "Remembering Delmore Schwartz" "Midnight Cinema" "Up All Night With A Headache" |
| *Live Magazine* | "An Erotic Memory Of New York in the 1980s" |
| *The Louisiana Review* | Parts I, V, VI, and X of "Swatches" |
| *Lummox* | "A Party For The View" |
| *Night Magazine* | "Bio-Regionalism" |
| *Pirogi* | "Malaysian Fishing Basket" |
| *Public Illuminations* | "Wet Hair" |
| *The Visionary* | "Byron To The Greek Committee" |

ISBN 978-0-9817678-1-9

Printed in the U.S.A.

Front Cover Collage: R J
Back Cover Author Photo: Don Snyder ©2003

*For My Parents*

# CONTENTS

AN EROTIC MEMORY OF NEW YORK / 1

A BAD RECORD / 2

A PARTY FOR THE VIEW / 3

MALAYSIAN FISHING BASKET / 4

MIDNIGHT CINEMAS / 5

WET HAIR / 6

BIO-REGIONALISM / 7

THIRD AVENUE AT NIGHT / 10

UP ALL NIGHT WITH A HEADACHE / 11

REMEMBERING DELMORE SCHWARTZ / 12

BLAZE STARR'S AUTOGRAPH / 13

BYRON TO THE GREEK COMMITTEE / 14

SWATCHES / 16

# AN EROTIC MEMORY OF NEW YORK IN THE 1980S

Twenty-five years later,
I can still count the number of cigarettes
You smoked on our first night together,
And see how many inches the bottom of
The window was left opened to let the smoke out,
As you sat naked in a chair.  The lights
From the street made shadows
That covered you in one long blanket
Of ink.  We talked about what kind
Of tattoos we would get and where
We would wear them.  The next night, we celebrated
New Year's Eve in an illegal tattoo parlor
On The Lower East Side picking out designs
I still have in mind.

# A BAD RECORD

Charlie Green froze to death in an alley.

Leon Rapollo threw his clarinet
Into the lake and eventually went insane.

Buddy Bolden died in an asylum.

Jelly Roll Morton died with two cars
Tied end to end, trying to get to Los Angeles.

Bix drank himself into the ground.

King Oliver, broke, sold potatoes from
A roadside farm stand.

Bob Call only recorded one solo record in his life:
*31 BLUES*.    This poem makes 32.

# A PARTY FOR THE VIEW

A Saturday night party and my friend
Tells me how annoying it is
To stand at her apartment windows
And have construction workers
Wave to her, pausing from
Their work of laying a concrete floor
For another Donald Trump building.
Her friends and the friends of friends,
Gather at the windows to look out,
Then turn back to continue a conversation,
Finish a drink, or eat something.
My friend is losing the
Space where pigeons flock,
An outdoor parking lot where
Cab drivers go to pee, the illuminated
Billboard sign for Ogilvy and Mather
That illuminates the sky above fifty-fifth
Street.  But an eighteen-story building will bring
Another view to wallpaper her windows with:
People in their apartments,
Watching television, watering flower pots,
Reading in their underwear,
Or studying their computer screens.
Below, on the street, I watch a homeless man
Crawl into a cardboard box for the night,
His shopping cart parked in a doorway.
After the party, my friend tells me how a
Group plans to go downstairs and paste Anarchist
Stickers on the two giant cranes that usurp
The street.  I plan to go too and bring my drink.

3

# MALAYSIAN FISHING BASKET
## *For Bob Ghiradella*

A survival tool from a culture
I know nothing about is now
A ten dollar decoration,
Lying on the floor
Of my favorite thrift shop,
Beneath a rack of cheap dresses.

What would I do with it, except
Tie a wire to it and hang it from the ceiling
Like a temple bell.   Far better,
To prop it up in a corner
Of my room and keep dirty laundry in it.

# MIDNIGHT CINEMAS

Then, it was midnight showings
Of double features,
Leaving the theater
At four o'clock in the morning,
Stopping to eat franks at a Forty Second
Street Nedick's stand more ancient
Than the Second World War.
One morning we watched a knife fight
While drinking our sodas.
The streets were threatening
With the thrill of living
On our own, without money.
The sex booths were cheap
But the night life cheaper because
It was free for the viewing.
Now, the buildings are torn down,
Or closed, looking as tired
As the acid-brown pages of 1950s
*Confidential* magazines in plastic.

# WET HAIR

Beneath an anthology of Chinese poems,
I found a letter from an old lover.
She writes to remind me to
Move the bed against the west
Wall, under the front window,
So the cigarette smoke won't
Smell-up the blankets.
Some mornings, she sat on
The edge of the bed,
And let me dry her hair
With a damp towel, plan
An early dinner, make small talk,
Or slip back into bed,
To fuck, before going to work.
The anthology was an unsigned gift,
To encourage me to write more
Poems about traveling, lost friends,
Money, dirty clothes, or being drunk in the rain.
I write her name on the inside, front cover,
Put the book on the bed, to read again,
And throw out the letter.

# BIO-REGIONALISM
### *For Leonard Kriegel*


I

Winter is ending late as I begin to
Walk around Chelsea only to find another
Apartment building is for sale,
And my Chinese laundry is closing,
Forced out of business by high rent,
New art galleries and boutiques.
I'm beginning to miss Eleventh Avenue's
Phantom world of ownerless shopping
Carts and aggressive transvestites,
The remnants of an unenclosed frontier.
Today, pots of English Ivy line the street
Outside the decorator's store.


II

A forecast of no snow has released
The city from a fear of more snow.
The streets around Twenty-third Street
Are busy with late evening traffic;
Salt on the concrete burns my dog's paws.
Some unemployed from the Welfare hotel
Stand on the corner, talking.
Two hours later, snow.
So much for weather reports.
The only mail I've gotten today is
One credit card offer and two
Postcards from an old girlfriend,
Writing about Lent.

III

A dead pigeon has fallen onto
The sign above the liquor store,
On my street. It hangs limp above the "Q."
The drug store where Mad Dog Coll
Was shot to death in a phone booth,
Has a sale on bottled water.


IV

April. This is the season when the trees
Between 8th and 9th Avenues,
On the north side of 23rd Street,
Begin to blossom. But since
The temperature is ninety,
Thirty degrees above normal,
A ban on outdoor watering is announced
On the radio. The view from my window,
Shows bare trees sticking out of
The concrete sidewalk.


V

April 24th. An early morning movie shoot in
The neighborhood on West 21st Street between
9th and 10th Ave. A no parking regulation
Has gone into effect. Woody Allen's spring project
Has transformed this block into a 1940s
Photograph. I think about my parents
Meeting at the NMU on West 17th Street.
I haven't been born yet.

## VI

I run my air conditioner at night
And recycle my garbage in the morning,
Wondering how much of a difference it makes.
The Bush administration
Doesn't recognize global warming,
So why should I feel guilty about
The melting polar ice caps while
I can still put ice in my dog's water bowl.
I used to enjoy the spring, but
Now I look forward to autumn;
It reminds me of Tolstoy's last letter.

# THIRD AVENUE AT NIGHT

I

One night at Sheehan's bar,
A man dropped dead.  He wasn't
A regular, just an occasional drinker,
But no one knew him.
Fortunately, the owner's son, a cop,
Was not there.  So, everyone
Waited until closing, then moved
The body outside, closed the door
And locked it.  When my father
Came home that morning,
He called the police to report the incident.

II

Six months later,
The landlord refused to renew
Sheehan's lease.  So, on
The last night, the regulars
Tore the place to pieces, ripping up
The bar and the pipes in the wall.
When the cops arrived,
The bar had emptied out and was locked up.
My mother was glad the place was gone.

# UP ALL NIGHT WITH A HEADACHE

4 A. M.  I find my notebook in the dark
And scribble this: couple living on the floor
Below, arguing.  My cat peeing in the bathroom
Sandbox sounds like a woman I once
Lived with.  The outside wall of my apt.
Creaks from a strong, winter wind,
Pushing against the bricks.  It's too early
To get a morning newspaper, so I find
Things to do.  Turn on the light:
White walls and a few photographs framed.
The bright light of a ceramic table lamp
Shines on living room details:
A six foot belt of ivy that
Laces my two windows, various leaves
Eaten by the cat, then vomited onto the floor,
Forming a hairball to be cleaned.
The contract to renew my rental lease
waits to be signed.
The piles of paper, new and old projects in different
States of completion; Goethe called writing,
"idle busyness."  Where does it end?
I wipe the dust off my mother's framed photo;
Write in my notebook calendar: Feb. 24th 1917;
Day great grandfather died from a yellow liver.
Drink a glass of water and get back into bed;
I'm my own last will and testament and
Think more about sex than actually get any.
This is only the second poem I've written this month,
There's something else I forgot to write down,
What was it?

# REMEMBERING DELMORE SCHWARTZ
## *For Elizabeth Pollet*

The first time I came to visit,
It was snowing outside and we
Watched the snow covering the
Remains of the old Westside docks:
Pile fields sticking out of the water.
You talked about living in New York
In the 1940s and being bohemian.
Like everyone else from that generation,
You mentioned how the art world was
Smaller then and people with strong
Opinions were cultural "heros."
The second time I came,
It was late spring and people were
Sunbathing on the lawn below your window.
You gave me a copy of the
Posthumous journals and I began
Reading them as you opened a bottle
Of wine.  I said, "Delmore had a great sense
Of humor."  And you laughed and said, "Sure did."
Now the summer is here and
I'm reading Schwartz's published letters.
The letters show him breaking up,
Drinking more, taking pills and
Writing people for money,
But his humor, apparently, never left him.
And I look at your printed photograph on a page,
Taken in the 1950s, when the marriage
Began to break up.  You were a beauty
With brains and a first novel just published,
Now, sadly, out of print.

# BLAZE STARR'S AUTOGRAPH

In the late 1930s,
After LaGuardia closed
The live burlesques houses
In New York, you had to go to
New Jersey to see the real thing.
But we had movies to watch:
The 42nd Street grind houses, open 24/7.
When I was old enough to visit one of
These theatres I saw lots of flesh and hips,
Like watching a meteor shower
In slow motion; things moving
Like gravity didn't exist,
I even forgot to blink.
Now I have her,
Poised and standing still
In an 8 x 10 glossy,
I just brought from an autograph dealer.
The famous tits
Unhidden behind black lingerie,
Lips open, garter belts tight
Yards of legs right down
To her high heels.
And at the bottom signed in blue ink,
"With love and kisses always".

# BYRON TO THE GREEK COMMITTEE
## *(circa 1826)*

I'm writing from a post-romantic city
Where your memory of paradise
Is stained by pollution and neglect.
Today, I live in an historical borough
Among partisans who speak an out-dated
Form of the language you fought and died for.
Money is always a problem and fundraising is hopeless.

*Many have turned away and given up, retreating to*
*Their gardens to live in an old lifestyle.*
*I too live with my recollections of the past;*
*The present facts supporting my return to your cause*
*Are constantly subverted by an undisciplined*
*Government that offers no interest or protection to*
*Someone interested in your salvation.*[1]

The venerable places have been razed
And replaced with shopping malls and high rises.
Now that the money is gone, ignorant barbarians
Overrun and devastate the country.
I hope I am not misunderstood in the history books,

*But the enthusiasm gathered around*
*The current despotism is*
*A nauseating development.*
*Members you chose now live without protection,*
*Doomed to indifference and torpidity,*
*A form of slavery of the spirit.*

My influence has been eliminated for the most part
From books and other records.
Nothing gets through that is not
Altered to suit the government's needs.
I sit and wait, reading about your continuing decline.
No one has taken the necessary actions,

*And if a thousand victories will not establish a tyrant,*
*Would a single defeat be his overthrow?*

---

1 All above quotes are from THE GREEK COMMITTEE: A
Summary Account of the Steam boats for Lord
Cochrane's Expedition: with some few words upon the
two Frigates ordered at New York, for the Service of
Greece. By Count Alerino Palma. London. 1820.
Published in THE WESTMINSTER REVIEW. Number VI.
July 1826. Pages 113-131

# SWATCHES

## I

I save samples of material, cut from
Hanging bolts of lace; washed
Chenille, Cotton apricot Jacq,
Ecru, Antique scroll Matelasse,
Cognac velultra, and other
Colors and patterns of textured swatches.
I keep them in a bowl on my table;
My oracle, to predict the kind of look
I want in my apartment,
An offering for stylish gods,
To find the right interior season.

## II

My apartment has a "lived-in look."
I own too many books, pictures,
And the inherited brick-a-brack
Of my parents' lives.
I live in Karma's museum,
With pieces of my personal history
Taking up space, interrupting the energy flow,
 As a Feng Shui master would see.

III

The clothes in my mother's closet
Were given away, to charities,
Or as gifts.  Now, strangers,
On the streets wear
Her colored suits, jackets, dresses.
These are people I'll never meet, and if I ever did,
What could they say to me?


IV

During the French Revolution,
The headless bodies of the aristocracy
Were dumped on carts, or left
In ditches.  After their heads were put on stakes,
Were their clothes taken
And sold, or cut into rags,
For maids to clean kitchens with?
I'm thinking about the material.


V

The lines in my hands are starting
To deepen into folds,
Dividing the present from the past.
In a dream, death is a back road in the early
Morning dark, as a Cadillac's
Headlights shine on some men making deals.
Their voices echoing against my spine.

VI

Once, on a tour, visiting Corinth,
I found a piece of pottery, among
The excavations; part of a rim of a large pot,
With the glaze still visible.  I left it there,
Not wanting to be arrested,
Or to carry anymore of the past
Than the picture postcards I found
In tourist shops.


VII

On my last visit to
Wetumpka, Alabama, during your funeral,
No one asked me any questions,
They just sat in the pews and
Cast long glances trying to figure out
Which side I came from.
There is one family grave left empty,
In the city cemetery, but it's not mine;
I don't even know who brought it.


VIII

Sunday, and spring again, as I'm waiting
In the ABC carpet store,
For one of the floor assistants to cut
Another swatch for me.  It's a style
I never saw before, without a name tag
To identify it, but I don't care,
I like the way it feels.

IX

Looking at three graces on a
Roman relief mirror doesn't inspire
Me, but more than the scholarly commentaries
Written on them, touching the stone does.


X

I'm walking on a street of scaffolds,
Our old neighborhood,
As the light shines in dirty puddles
Of acid water, leftover from
Hoses blasting clean the brick surfaces
Of the building where our studio
Apartment, now renovated, is being shown.
Apartment hunters line the
Entrance, waiting for their turn to
Intrude on my reflections of our past life together;
I moved out, you stayed
And found a new partner, but still
Had sex with me—until the final breakup.
I'm tempted to see the place one more time,
But don't. I cross the street and walk home.


XI

I just threw out my collection
Of swatches. They were beautiful,
But I needed to clear my table.

www.ingramcontent.com/pod-product-compliance
Lightning Source LLC
Chambersburg PA
CBHW061800040426
42447CB00011B/2393